Have a Great Day!

The Story of Jesus and Zacchaeus

We are grateful to the following team of authors for their contributions to *God Loves Me*, a Bible story program for young children. This Bible story, one of a series of fifty-two, was written by Patricia L. Nederveld, managing editor for CRC Publications. Suggestions for using this book were developed by Sherry Ten Clay, training coordinator for CRC Publications and freelance author from Albuquerque, New Mexico. Yvonne Van Ee, an early childhood educator, served as project consultant and wrote *God Loves Me*, the program guide that accompanies this series of Bible storybooks.

Nederveld has served as a consultant to Title I early childhood programs in Colorado. She has extensive experience as a writer, teacher, and consultant for federally funded preschool, kindergarten, and early childhood programs in Colorado, Texas, Michigan, Florida, Missouri, and Washington, using the *High/Scope* Education Research Foundation curriculum. In addition to writing the *Bible Footprints* church curriculum for four- and five-year-olds, Nederveld edited the revised *Threes* curriculum and the first edition of preschool through second grade materials for the *LiFE* curriculum, all published by CRC Publications.

Ten Clay taught preschool for ten years in public schools in California, Missouri, and North Carolina and served as a Title IV preschool teacher consultant in Kansas City. For over twenty-five years she has served as a church preschool leader and also as a MOPS (Mothers of Preschoolers) volunteer. Ten Clay is coauthor of the preschool-kindergarten materials of the *LiFE* curriculum published by CRC Publications.

Van Ee is a professor and early childhood program advisor in the Education Department at Calvin College, Grand Rapids, Michigan. She has served as curriculum author and consultant for Christian Schools International and wrote the original *Story Hour* organization manual and curriculum materials for fours and fives.

Photo on page 5: Digital Stock Images; photo on page 20: Peter Cade/Tony Stone Images.

Library of Congress Cataloging-in-Publication Data

Nederveld, Patricia L., 1944-
    Have a great day!: the story of Jesus and Zacchaeus/Patricia L. Nederveld.
        p. cm. — (God loves me; bk. 41)
      Summary: Retells the Bible story about the dishonest tax collector Zacchaeus
and how he is changed when he meets Jesus. Includes follow-up activities.
      ISBN 1-56212-310-6
      1. Zacchaeus (Biblical character)—Juvenile literature. [1. Zacchaeus (Biblical
character). 2. Bible stories—N.T.] I. Title. II. Series: Nederveld, Patricia L., 1944-
God loves me; bk. 41.
BS2520.Z3N43   1998
232.9'5—dc21
                                    98-15642
                                      CIP
                                      AC

10 9 8 7 6 5 4 3 2 1

Have a Great Day!

The Story of Jesus and Zacchaeus

PATRICIA L. NEDERVELD

ILLUSTRATIONS BY PATRICK KELLEY

CRC Publications
Grand Rapids, Michigan

This is a story from God's book, the Bible.

It's for say name(s) of your child(ren).
It's for me too!

Luke 19:1-10

Most days were *not* great days for Zacchaeus. Most days were pretty bad! You see, Zacchaeus had a job that made everyone hate him.

I wonder what kind of day Zacchaeus is having today?

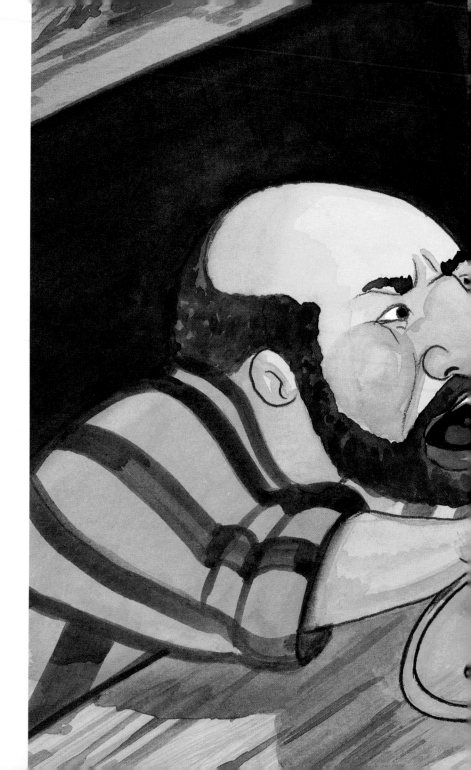

Y
es! It looks like another bad day!

"Zacchaeus, every day you take our money for the king. But you take too much. We think you keep too much for yourself!" the people grumbled. "That's wrong!"

Then someone shouted, "Jesus is coming!" and everyone ran to see him. Zacchaeus wanted to see Jesus too. But today was a really bad day—Zacchaeus was just too short to see over everyone else.

But Zacchaeus didn't give up. He ran ahead and climbed a tree. Zacchaeus watched as the crowd of people came closer and closer.

When the crowd got to the tree, Jesus stopped. He looked up, straight at Zacchaeus. "Zacchaeus, come down! I want to go to your house today!" Jesus said.

"Welcome to my house!" said Zacchaeus with a smile. Jesus looked happy too. But the people who watched wondered why Jesus wanted to visit someone who took their money and kept it for himself.

"Jesus, I want to give back all the money I took from people. From now on I just want to be kind to everyone," said Zacchaeus.

"Your life has been changed today, Zacchaeus!" said Jesus. And he smiled at Zacchaeus. "This is a *great* day, Zacchaeus!"

I wonder if you know that Jesus always loves you . . .

Dear Jesus, thank you for loving us all the time. We love you, Jesus. Amen.

Suggestions for Follow-up

Opening

Greet your little ones today with joy and excitement. Let them know how happy you are that Jesus loves you—and each one of them too! Invite each child to join you in greeting the others as they arrive.

Gather the children around you as you prepare to tell the story. Sing "Jesus Loves Me" (Songs Section, *God Loves Me* program guide). Wonder with the children about the person Jesus loved in the Bible story you're going to tell—was this person big or small? Short or tall? Good or bad? Sad or happy?

Learning Through Play

Learning through play is the best way! The following activity suggestions are meant to help you provide props and experiences that will invite the children to play their way into the Scripture story and its simple truth. Try to provide plenty of time for the children to choose their own activities and to play individually. Use group activities sparingly—little ones learn most comfortably with a minimum of structure.

1. Provide a low step stool or other stable surface for little ones who want to pretend to be Zacchaeus climbing up to see Jesus. You might want to place the stool behind a sturdy box so children can climb up and peek over the edge. If you wish, place a picture of Jesus inside the box. Station a helper close by to help your eager climbers.

2. Supply your art area with crayons, simple tree shapes, and Zacchaeus figures (see Pattern R, Patterns Section, *God Loves Me* program guide). Invite children to scribble color the trees. Provide small containers of colorful dry cereal, and dot each child's tree with a few drops of glue. Show your little ones how to stick the cereal in the glue. (You'll want extra cereal for snacking!) Add a few more drops of glue, and help children place Zacchaeus in the tree. Ask them to tell you why Zacchaeus was up in the tree. Who came by? Express joy as you remind them that Jesus loved Zacchaeus and that he loves them too.

3. Ask parents and friends to save metal lids from frozen juice cans. These can be used as giant pieces of money. Provide large coffee cans or plastic containers so your little ones can collect money from you and give it back as Zacchaeus did. They'll enjoy filling and dumping as you talk about what Zacchaeus did before and after he saw Jesus. Help them express the feelings of the people and Zacchaeus.

4. Sing or say "Jesus Is a Friend of Mine" (Songs Section, *God Loves Me* program guide) as children mimic your actions:

Jesus is a friend of mine.
Praise him. (clap, clap)
Jesus is a friend of mine.
Praise him. (clap, clap)
Praise him. (clap, clap)
Praise him. (clap, clap)
Jesus is a friend of mine.
Praise him. (clap, clap)

If you prefer, use rhythm instruments, bells, or party horns or substitute other actions for the clapping.

5. Let your little ones help decorate your snack table with colorful streamers and party napkins. Play a recording of their favorite gospel songs. Serve a special treat, and wonder with the children what Zacchaeus served for dinner. Talk about how happy Zacchaeus was that Jesus came to his house. Celebrate Jesus' love!

Closing

Gather the children around you with a reminder that Jesus loves us every day—on bad days (*hang your head sadly*), on good days (*clap your hands*), on sad days (*frown*), and on happy days (*smile*). If you wish, repeat the days and actions, and invite your little ones to do the actions. Express joy again that Jesus loves you and [name each child]. Say the prayer on page 21 as you give a group hug.

At Home

A peaceful, sleeping child; a warm, sunny day; a party around the kitchen table—these things fill our hearts with joy and a sense of Jesus' presence in our homes. How about spilt milk, angry words, a temper tantrum, a late start? Yes, Jesus is with us then too—he loves us always! Look for ways to remind your little one of Jesus' unending love. You might try the words and actions described in the closing activity. If this becomes a routine in your home, don't be surprised if your little one senses your own need for a reminder that Jesus loves you too!

Old Testament Stories

Blue and Green and Purple Too! *The Story of God's Colorful World*

It's a Noisy Place! *The Story of the First Creatures*

Adam and Eve *The Story of the First Man and Woman*

Take Good Care of My World! *The Story of Adam and Eve in the Garden*

A Very Sad Day *The Story of Adam and Eve's Disobedience*

A Rainy, Rainy Day *The Story of Noah*

Count the Stars! *The Story of God's Promise to Abraham and Sarah*

A Girl Named Rebekah *The Story of God's Answer to Abraham*

Two Coats for Joseph *The Story of Young Joseph*

Plenty to Eat *The Story of Joseph and His Brothers*

Safe in a Basket *The Story of Baby Moses*

I'll Do It! *The Story of Moses and the Burning Bush*

Safe at Last! *The Story of Moses and the Red Sea*

What Is It? *The Story of Manna in the Desert*

A Tall Wall *The Story of Jericho*

A Baby for Hannah *The Story of an Answered Prayer*

Samuel! Samuel! *The Story of God's Call to Samuel*

Lions and Bears! *The Story of David the Shepherd Boy*

David and the Giant *The Story of David and Goliath*

A Little Jar of Oil *The Story of Elisha and the Widow*

One, Two, Three, Four, Five, Six, Seven! *The Story of Elisha and Naaman*

A Big Fish Story *The Story of Jonah*

Lions, Lions! *The Story of Daniel*

New Testament Stories

Jesus Is Born! *The Story of Christmas*

Good News! *The Story of the Shepherds*

An Amazing Star! *The Story of the Wise Men*

Waiting, Waiting, Waiting! *The Story of Simeon and Anna*

Who Is This Child? *The Story of Jesus in the Temple*

Follow Me! *The Story of Jesus and His Twelve Helpers*

The Greatest Gift *The Story of Jesus and the Woman at the Well*

A Father's Wish *The Story of Jesus and a Little Boy*

Just Believe! *The Story of Jesus and a Little Girl*

Get Up and Walk! *The Story of Jesus and a Man Who Couldn't Walk*

A Little Lunch *The Story of Jesus and a Hungry Crowd*

A Scary Storm *The Story of Jesus and a Stormy Sea*

Thank You, Jesus! *The Story of Jesus and One Thankful Man*

A Wonderful Sight! *The Story of Jesus and a Man Who Couldn't See*

A Better Thing to Do *The Story of Jesus and Mary and Martha*

A Lost Lamb *The Story of the Good Shepherd*

Come to Me! *The Story of Jesus and the Children*

Have a Great Day! *The Story of Jesus and Zacchaeus*

I Love You, Jesus! *The Story of Mary's Gift to Jesus*

Hosanna! *The Story of Palm Sunday*

The Best Day Ever! *The Story of Easter*

Goodbye—for Now *The Story of Jesus' Return to Heaven*

A Prayer for Peter *The Story of Peter in Prison*

Sad Day, Happy Day! *The Story of Peter and Dorcas*

A New Friend *The Story of Paul's Conversion*

Over the Wall *The Story of Paul's Escape in a Basket*

A Song in the Night *The Story of Paul and Silas in Prison*

A Ride in the Night *The Story of Paul's Escape on Horseback*

The Shipwreck *The Story of Paul's Rescue at Sea*

Holiday Stories

Selected stories from the New Testament to help you celebrate the Christian year

Jesus Is Born! *The Story of Christmas*

Good News! *The Story of the Shepherds*

An Amazing Star! *The Story of the Wise Men*

Hosanna! *The Story of Palm Sunday*

The Best Day Ever! *The Story of Easter*

Goodbye—for Now *The Story of Jesus' Return to Heaven*

These fifty-two books are the heart of *God Loves Me*, a Bible story program designed for young children. Individual books (or the entire set) and the accompanying program guide *God Loves Me* are available from CRC Publications (1-800-333-8300).